How To Write Specifications

This booklet serves as a guide to preparing a specification document and what should or shouldn't be included. The booklet outlines the general principles of specification writing. However, due to the enormous range of the goods and services available, it is not possible to detail every particular type of specification.

Published by KREAV Publishing

ISBN 978-0-646-31599-7

3rd Edition

PO Box 6064 Griffith
ACT 2603
Australia

Illustrated by Heath Schauer

Edited by Jane Schauer

Contents

Section 1

Introduction

In this section:

- **The specification defined**

- **Types of specifications**

PROVIDE ENOUGH DETAIL

1. Introduction

A Specification is...

When you want to procure some goods or services, you need to describe your requirements so that the correct goods or services can be obtained.

A specification defines your requirements so that the supplier knows what to provide. The specification, therefore, needs to be written in such a clear manner that you get the correct goods or services and the supplier is able to satisfactorily fill the order quickly and confidently.

In fact the success or failure of obtaining the needed goods or services (the procurement process), depends largely on the specification document. It should clearly reflect a true and accurate statement of requirements of what is required.

Notes

Specification Types

Specification documents often describe the following three requirements:

✍ Functional Requirement

The information in the functional requirement defines the job to be performed by the product, for example - a computerised accounting system.

✍ Performance Requirement

The performance requirement information is an extension of the information provided in the functional requirement description. The description of the performance requirement provides such details as maximum and minimum performance criteria and methods of measuring this performance. However, it does not state how to achieve this performance, (which gives potential suppliers the ability to innovate to meet the requirement).

✍ Technical Requirement

Extra technical information is sometimes required to help clarify what you want. Technical requirements can describe such criteria as size, capacity, power consumption, tolerances and materials. Technical drawings can also be included to help clarification.

Section 2

Foundation Rules

In this section

- **Basic requirements for creating specifications**

Notes

2. Foundation

Basic Requirements

Simple specifications can combine all three types of specifications (functional, performance and technical) in the one document. Combinations, such as function and performance, are also acceptable. More complex specifications may require separate sections in the document to help more clearly define requirements. Whether simple or complex, you must decide which topics to include when developing your specification document.

In addition, there are some rules to apply for any specification document, no matter how simple or complex.

The rules are:

1. State your requirements clearly, so that the reader is in no doubt as to what is to be provided.

2. Give sufficient information to enable suppliers to accurately cost the goods or services to be supplied.

3. Clearly explain the means to be used to evaluate the offered goods or services. For example, your criteria for examination and testing must be clear.

4. Avoid over specifying. Your specification should contain the essential features only.

5. As far as practical, ensure your specification provides for equal opportunity for all potential suppliers to satisfy it.

Section 3

Research

In this section

- **Importance of clarity**

- **Getting input from the end user**

- **Consulting with potential suppliers**

- **Keeping confidentiality**

Notes

3. Research

Development of Specifications

The development of specifications involves more than just the writer.

It is preferable that the writers of specifications are the users of the goods or services to be provided, as they should have a clear understanding of their needs. However, the end users are not always the writers, because of various reasons, such as they may not have the required writing skills. If you are the designated specification writer, but not the end user of the goods or services, it is essential that you consult in depth with the user to fully understand their requirements.

All specifications should contain only essential information and be easy to read and understand. They should be logical and clear and it should be easy to locate specific information in them.

Research has found that most readers consider a clear style to be one that has:

- short sentences (average of 22 words);

- simple words (eg cats rather than felines);

- active voice rather than passive voice (eg "provide clear instructions", rather than "clear instructions should be provided");

- short paragraphs (average 75 words);

- Arabic rather than Roman numerals (eg 2 rather than II).

To avoid confusing your reader, it is important that you continue to use the same word each time you mention a piece of equipment, or process. For example, always use the term "white board marker", rather than varying the term and sometimes calling the item a "texter", sometimes a "marker pen", and sometimes a "white board marker".

If your organisation has any procurement staff, consult them. Your procurement staff could provide assistance by supplying previous specifications, advising about purchasing and procurement methods, or helping with market research and an acquisition strategy.

Also consult relevant people in the industry which supplies the goods/services about such issues as what is possible etc. Such consultation will help you shape a realistic specification which should result in competitive tenders.

After you have done several drafts of your specification document, you may need to again consult with the potential suppliers to further refine your draft. If you have been fair and ethical in the consultation process, the specification document usually will reflect a wide procurement opportunity, rather than favouring one potential supplier.

An important ethic is to always respect confidential information.

Notes

Section 4

Structure & Content

In this section

- **Building the structure - eight simple rules**

- **What to avoid**

- **Who should check your document**

- **What content to put in your document**

- **Ordering your content**

AVOID JARGON

4. Structure & Content

Structure of Specifications

Here are some simple rules to ensure the document meets the minimum structure requirements of most simple and complex specifications:

✓ **In each section, list most important things first**

✓ **Use simple language**

✓ **Avoid jargon**

✓ **Define any unusual terms and acronyms (eg W.H.O. means World Health Organisation)**

✓ **Create a logical structure - start and finish**

✓ **Avoid repetition of information**

✓ **Layout document neatly**

✓ **Use numbered paragraphs unless your specification is very simple (numbers assist discussion)**

Avoid having long, unsorted lists of requirements. These can be quite confusing to readers. Sort your information into categories and, if necessary, subcategories. Then present shorter lists, under suitable category or subcategory headings.

It may be helpful to have the document edited by someone as it is developed. Choose someone unfamiliar with the requirement, so they can edit the specification to make sure it is easy to understand. In addition, discuss drafts with the end user(s) of the goods or services to be supplied, and also those responsible for the actual procurement.

In your draft allow for additional information to be included. For example, the procurement staff may need contractual clauses; users may require some technical detail to be included for specific applications.

Unless they help clarify the requirement, avoid including information from such documents as offer or contract documents.

Content of Specifications

The document should follow the following basic structure, though not all sections are always needed.

✓ **Cover sheet**

✓ **Title**

    ✓ **Table of contents**

    ✓ **Glossary of terms and acronyms**

✓ **Introduction**

✓ **Background information and history**

✓ **Scope of requirements**

    ✓ **List of associated publications/ standards**

    ✓ **External approvals required**

    ✓ **Security considerations**

    ✓ **Environmental, ergonomic considerations**

✓ **Detailed requirements, including functional, performance and technical characteristics**

    ✓ **On going support considerations**

    ✓ **Marking of goods supplied**

    ✓ **Packaging**

    ✓ **Quality management**

✓ **Testing to be applied**

Notes

Section 5

Finishing Touches

In this section:

- **Testing specifications**

- **Getting approval**

- **Organising your material**

- **Following-up**

Notes

5. Finishing Touches

Testing Specifications

Test the final draft of your specification to ensure potential suppliers will be able to:

- easily and quickly locate information;

- understand explanations.

Your test readers should have the same sort of knowledge level as the intended final readers of your specification (your potential suppliers).

Have at least two test readers review your document and make notes on it about:

- any confusing sentences or sections;

- information they think is missing;

- how it might be improved.

Once you receive your test readers' feedback you may need to do another draft and then have that tested.

Approval of Specifications

The final draft of a specification document will normally be subject to approval by the management of the company that issues the specification. They should:

- certify accuracy of the information;

- ensure the requirements are effectively defined;

- confirm that the specification is free from bias towards one, or a limited group of suppliers;

- confirm that they accept responsibility for the specification.

Organising Your Documents

Issue a unique specification document number, retain and file a copy.

DESCRIBE VARIATIONS REQUIRED

After Procurement

Once the specification has been issued and the goods or services have been supplied, installed, tested and accepted, there are a number of follow up actions which you, as the specification document writer, should ideally undertake:

✓ **Review the document**

Learn from any mistakes (particularly any problems with the definition of requirements).

✓ **Revise the specification document**

Any weaknesses of the original document can now be amended to assist future specification writing.

✓ **File original and revised versions**

This is especially recommended for frequent purchases, because the filed examples will assist with the writing of similar future specifications.

✓ **Ensure the file is available to everyone involved**

You might even chose to circulate it for comment. You may receive helpful or important feedback from users and procurement staff.

Section 6

Help -

Examples and Checklists

In this section:

- **Specification questionnaire and plan**

- **Specification content checklist and revision checklist**

- **Specification example**

Notes

6. Help

Preliminary Questionnaire

Answering these questions before you write your specification will:

- *help your write an effective specification*
- *assist another writer if they have to finish the specification for you*

1. What type of specification are you writing? _____

   _____

2. Why is it important? _____

   _____

3. Who will be your readers?

   main   _____

   other   _____

(questionnaire continues on the next page)

4. When must your specification be complete and printed ready for distribution?

   _____

5. What type of design or format will present your information most effectively?

   _____

   _____

6. Who can you contact for advice regarding necessary content?

   in your organisation_____

   potential suppliers _____

7. Who will proofread your document?

   _____

8. Who will be included in the specification as the contact to answer questions?

   _____

Production Plan

Creating a production plan will assist you to stay on track with the development and use of your specification.

When do you need to have the following completed?

1. First draft _____

2. Proofreading _____

3. Second draft _____

4. Testing your draft on people with same characteristics as end readers

   _____

5. Final draft _____

6. Printing _____

7. Re-evaluation after use, revision and archiving

   _____

(questionnaire continues on the next page)

8. List any resources you will require to produce your
   specification _____

   _____

   _____

   _____

   _____

   _____

Specification Content Checklist

Use this checklist once you have written your specification, to ensure it contains all the information it needs. Your specification may not need all the sections listed below; however, the checklist helps insure you have not forgotten to include any information you should have included.

☐ Cover sheet

☐ Title

    ☐ Table of contents

    ☐ Glossary of terms and acronyms

☐ Introduction

    ☐ Background information and history

☐ Scope of requirements

    ☐ List of associated publications/standards

    ☐ External approvals required

    ☐ Security considerations

    ☐ Environmental, ergonomic considerations

(checklist continues on the next page)

☐ Detailed requirements specification (including functional, performance and technical characteristics)

☐ On-going support considerations

☐ Marking of goods supplied

☐ Packaging

☐ Quality management

☐ Testing information

Revision Checklist

☐ Input was gathered from users/suppliers

☐ Information is clear and easy to understand

☐ Information is presented in a logical order

☐ All acronyms and unusual terms are defined

☐ Same word is used each time to describe each piece of equipment or process

☐ Document has been spell checked

☐ Document includes contact name and phone number for queries

☐ Document has been tested and then revised

Notes

Specification Example

The following is an example of a specification document.

Bonza Pty Ltd

Address _____

Phone _____

Fax _____

Email _____

Specification For

A Home Office Automated Fax/Modem System

Date_____

Spec. Number 1/20xx

Contact Officer:
Joe Smith (Phone xxxxxxxx ext 451)

Notes

Specification For A Home Office Automated Fax-modem System

Table of Contents

List of definitions and abbreviations

WORLDTEL	World Telecommunications
FAX	Facsimile
Gb	Giga Byte (one billion bytes)

Introduction

Due to the expansion of business, Bonza Pty Ltd wishes to upgrade its system of sending and receiving faxes via a computer and fax-modem.

Background Information

In 2010, Bonza Pty Ltd was contracted to instruct various government departments in effective writing and authoring of technical manuals. Due to the success of these classes, the business of teaching technical writing expanded rapidly. This has created a need to improve the methods of communication used by the business.

Many of Bonza's clients communicate by email; however, some still prefer to send faxes. Bonza Pty Ltd wants to upgrade from its current fax machine which has no computer connectivity to one that has computer connectivity. The new fax system machine will send documents to clients and potential clients from files stored on the Apple Macintosh computer system used in the office.

The new fax system should also allow faxes
received by the computer system to be stored
in a data file, for perusal and action at the
convenience of office staff. It is intended that
messages received be checked daily, and those
requiring immediate action be printed out on a
laser printer connected to the computer system.
Those messages of a non urgent nature will be
filed away into data files for later action and/
or archiving.

Transmissions of messages will also come
from these data files. The documents to be
transmitted will be prepared in advance and
sent directly from a computer by commands from
the keyboard and mouse.

Scope

The requirement is for:

- A fax/modem, capable of connection to
  the existing WORLDTEL phone socket where
  the existing fax machine is connected.

- Appropriate software to receive fax
  messages through the communication
  port in the computer's back plane.

- Appropriate software to select text
  files from any directory located on
  the computer's storage devices,
  then to have those files sent to a
  receiving fax. Any file's size will
  not exceed 100 pages of A4 text.

The supplier will be required to provide the following services to Bonza Pty Ltd:

- supply and deliver the hardware;

- supply and deliver the software;

- supply installation and set-up;

- supply documentation.

The supplier will be required to demonstrate the system to office staff once installation is complete.

The supplier will provide on-site service during the warranty period, and specify conditions for out of warranty service and support. Any extra services or components not considered part of the requirement, but which the supplier sees as necessary, will be provided as a separate attachment. This includes energy or other services not available on site, but necessary for the requirement.

List of Applicable Documents

- Specification number 1/20xx, specification for the supply of computer equipment to Bonza Pty. Ltd.

- Macintosh system manuals for the computer system fitted.

- WORLDTEL standards for telephone services.

External Approvals

The supplier will provide information of any approvals required by Telstra, Optus or WORLDTEL phone companies to install the system as required. This information will cover:

- the work needing approval;

- the relevant authority issuing such approvals;

- time delays predicted to obtain such approvals;

- the certification provided by such approvals.

Security Measures

The software and documentation should include security of data procedures for transmission, reception and storing of fax messages.

Environmental/Ergonomic Limitations

The system is to be installed in an air-conditioned office and located on the same platform as the computer system. The supplier will point out any operator functions requiring physical space.

Any requirements for adaptability and/or compatibility with existing equipment is to be furnished by the supplier.

Detailed Requirements

Functional Characteristics

The equipment, once installed, will be required
to receive fax messages at any time of the day
or night, because overseas messages will be
sent from widely varying time zones. The faxes
will not be immediately printed out, but stored
in a directory on the computer until required.
Fax messages will be sent at any time of the
day and night from files in the same directory
on the computer.

A list of telephone numbers will become an
integral part of the fax messaging system.
The number to be called will be selected from
the list, and the selected file will then be
transmitted.

Performance Characteristics

There shall be no reduction in message speed
from the existing system of a stand-alone fax.

Technical Characteristics

Storage space for messages will be supplied and
maintained on the existing Macintosh computer
system server, currently indicating free space
of 200 Gb. At regular intervals, files will
be archived and stored on portable storage
divices; this process must be supported by the
supplied software.

Message transmission should follow the existing "drag and drop" methods used with the Macintosh user interface. However, other forms of message handling will be considered.

Other Aspects

Supplied documentation should enable office staff to operate and maintain the system in accordance with this specification. The same documentation should also permit a limited amount of troubleshooting by office staff. Operating instructions should be short and easy to follow.

Support

The supplier should provide information on future upgrades, availability of software and hardware support and details of on and off site maintenance and repair facilities.

Markings

There will be a requirement for security markings on all hardware installed. For insurance purposes, the markings should be consistent with those on existing equipment. The existing markings on off the shelf equipment must have a minimum of:

- manufacturer;

- serial number;

- model number;

- item name;

- energy requirements;

- warnings.

Quality

The supplier should state their standards of Quality Management. The following standards are an example only:

- ISO 9001 Quality Management Systems

- ISO/IEC 26514:2008 System And Software Engineering Requirements For Designers & Developers Of User Documentation

Testing

The system will undergo the following testing once installed. Only upon satisfactory completion of the tests will the goods be accepted.

1. Simple "ON-OFF" switching of all required electrical power.

2. Starting of the computer system free from abnormal interruptions or messages.

3. Successful transmission of a five page document to three fax numbers.

4. Successful reception of the same, or equivalent, faxes from three fax calls.

5. Quick and easy storage of the same three faxes into allocated areas of the Bonza Pty Ltd server's hard disc storage.

6. Error-free reproduction of the documents on the Bonza Pty Ltd laser printer.

The tests may be carried out by the installation personnel; however, external testing personnel may be required by the purchaser.